THE HYPNOTIC GASTRIC BAND

For more information on Paul McKenna and his books,
see his website at www.paulmckenna.com

www.**rbooks**.co.uk

Also by Paul McKenna

I CAN MAKE YOU SMARTER

I CAN MAKE YOU HAPPY

I CAN MAKE YOU THIN

I CAN MAKE YOU THIN: 90-DAY SUCCESS JOURNAL

I CAN MAKE YOU THIN: LOVE FOOD, LOSE WEIGHT! (illustrated)

CONTROL STRESS

I CAN MAKE YOU SLEEP

I CAN MAKE YOU RICH

QUIT SMOKING TODAY

INSTANT CONFIDENCE

CHANGE YOUR LIFE IN SEVEN DAYS

I CAN MEND YOUR BROKEN HEART (with Hugh Willbourn)

THE HYPNOTIC WORLD OF PAUL McKENNA

THE HYPNOTIC GASTRIC BAND

•

PAUL McKENNA PH.D.

EDITED BY HUGH WILLBOURN PH.D.

BANTAM PRESS

LONDON · TORONTO · SYDNEY · AUCKLAND · JOHANNESBURG

TRANSWORLD PUBLISHERS
61–63 Uxbridge Road, London W5 5SA
A Random House Group Company
www.transworldbooks.co.uk

First published in Great Britain
in 2013 by Bantam Press
an imprint of Transworld Publishers

A CIP catalogue record for this book is available from the British Library.

ISBN 9780593070741

Addresses for Random House Group Ltd companies outside the UK
can be found at: www.randomhouse.co.uk
The Random House Group Ltd Reg. No. 954009

The Random House Group Limited supports the Forest Stewardship Council (FSC®), the
leading international forest-certification organization. Our books carrying the FSC
label are printed on FSC®-certified paper. FSC is the only forest-certification scheme
endorsed by the leading environmental organizations, including Greenpeace. Our
paper procurement policy can be found at www.randomhouse.co.uk/environment.

Designed and typeset by Julia Lloyd
Printed and bound in Great Britain by
Clays Ltd, Bungay, Suffolk

4 6 8 10 9 7 5 3

Mixed Sources
Product group from well-managed
forests and other controlled sources
www.fsc.org   Cert no. TT-COC-2139
© 1996 Forest Stewardship Council
FSC

CONTENTS

HOW TO USE THIS SYSTEM TO FIT YOUR HYPNOTIC GASTRIC BAND

Quick start instructions

This is more than a book. When you read this text, listen to the CD and watch the DVD:

> **you will install a hypnotic gastric band**
> **which will limit your eating...**

> **you will learn simple procedures**
> **which change how you feel...**

> **and you will prepare yourself to be happy**
> **and relaxed as a thin person.**

> **All you need to do is read the book**
> **and follow all the instructions**
> **carefully and completely.**

Installation

Installation Step 1

Read the book from start to finish. Follow the pre-operative instructions on page 67 and practise the exercises on pages 116, 128 and 130.

You can read this book and re-read it as many times as you want.

Installation Step 2

Watch the Havening DVD and practise the technique until you know it by heart.

Installation Step 3

Listen to Track 1 on the CD: Pre-operative instructions.

You can listen to this as many times as you wish.

Installation Step 4

Listen to Track 2: the Gastric Band Installation Trance.

Choose a time and a place where you can be quiet and undisturbed for half an hour to listen to the trance. After listening to the trance, avoid strenuous exercise for the rest of the day.

Remember, you must read the book from cover to cover before using the DVD or CD.

Maintenance

Maintenance Step 1

Listen to the Gastric Band Installation Trance to adjust your band at least once a month until you have maintained your target weight for at least six months.

Maintenance Step 2

Re-read the book and listen to the CD Pre-operative Track 1 as often as you wish to get a boost of positive reinforcement.

Maintenance Step 3

Keep practising the Havening technique (the DVD, and A Safe Haven on book page 116) and use it whenever you need to reduce stressful emotions or improve your well-being.

Maintenance Step 4

Follow the Four Golden Rules on pages 83–103. Most importantly, remember always to **eat consciously**. When you eat, focus on your food, feel pleasure and be aware of the signals from your body. This permits you to experience the fullness created by your hypnotic gastric band and enjoy every mouthful you eat.

THE HYPNOTIC GASTRIC BAND

•

CHAPTER ONE

Introducing your Hypnotic Gastric Band

Introducing your Hypnotic Gastric Band

I can only describe what you are about to experience as the closest thing to real magic I have ever witnessed. Of course, it's not magic, it's a scientific procedure, but the results are like magic. Imagine this: you listen to an audio programme, you can be as sceptical as you like, and suddenly your eating habits start to change. You eat less, you leave food on your plate and you don't feel like you are missing out. If you try to eat more, your body won't let you. It makes you feel full or even nauseous if you try to override it. The weight drops off. You feel an overwhelming sense of liberation and it almost seems too good to be true!

Yes, I didn't believe it either! But I have spent the last two years researching this extraordinary process with some of the world's leading scientific minds in weight loss, and I have used it successfully again and again, even with people who were supposedly 'impossible' cases. The continued repetition of this astounding success has led me to write this book. I don't see weight loss just as a business. To me it is one of the most powerful ways people can increase their health and happiness. I want everyone who uses my system to lose weight permanently so the whole crazy diet industry collapses. Of all the things I am able to help people with, weight loss is the one I feel most passionate about. That's why the hypnotic gastric band means so much to me. I think it's going to change the lives of millions of people around the world.

So, welcome to an amazing journey! You have just begun to change permanently how you eat. Your hypnotic gastric band will restrict your stomach and make you feel full so that you cannot eat large portions, and yet at the same time you will feel completely satisfied.

A gastric band is a radical surgical operation that reduces the available space in your stomach. A hypnotic gastric band is a psychological procedure that convinces your unconscious mind that you have had a gastric band fitted, so your body behaves exactly as if you have a gastric band.

A hypnotic gastric band is the perfect booster for you if:

you need to lose more than 30 pounds to achieve a slim, healthy body weight,

or

you have always been overweight,

or

you have lost weight by dieting in the past and subsequently put it all back on again and more,

or

you have found it difficult to recognize the moment when your body is telling you that you have eaten enough.

Satisfaction

You will feel completely satisfied by much, much smaller portions. Your stomach will tell you, 'Thanks very much, I'm full.' Your appetite will be physically changed. So you will lose weight until your body reaches a natural slim and healthy size. Throughout the process, even though you eat less, you will enjoy your food, make nourishing and healthy choices and get all the vitamins, protein, fibre and energy your body needs.

That may sound complicated, miraculous or unbelievable, but it is all down to one thing – a hypnotic operation which not only physically restricts your stomach but also resets the natural signalling system of your body so your brain knows when you have had enough to eat.

You don't have to worry about dieting or calorie counting, or meal substitutes, or 'good' foods and 'bad' foods, you will simply find smaller portions completely satisfying and your tastes will change so that you naturally seek out the healthy nourishment your body requires.

You will discover that often you do not feel able to finish what is on your plate. On the contrary, your body will give you a very clear, undeniable signal that you have had plenty to eat long before the plate is cleared.

When you reach your natural, healthy body weight, the same hypnotic process will adjust your gastric band so that you continue to get all the nourishment your body requires, and you will feel so satisfied that you cannot face eating any more than you really need.

As you lose weight, many other positive changes will be released into your life. And how does all this happen? All you have to do is follow the instructions in this book, listen to the CD and and watch the DVD.

Why this book?

In 2005 I wrote *I Can Make You Thin*. This was the summation of twenty years of research and I am proud to say it is the bestselling weight-loss book in British history. It has now been translated into thirty-five languages around the world. It has also been imitated by many other authors and organizations.

The book explains the Four Golden Rules of losing weight and it totally changed attitudes to weight loss. Permanent, healthy weight loss is not achieved through dieting. It is not about avoiding certain foods or buying expensive, artificial food substitutes. Losing weight successfully, and keeping it off, is done by restoring your sensitivity to the intelligence of your body. You can eat anything you want when you know how not to eat to excess. And you only eat when you are hungry.

I Can Make You Thin was an instant bestseller. Seven out of ten people who use the book lose weight. In other words, over the long-term, the success rate is more than six times the success rate of dieting and diet clubs. It is the most successful weight-loss programme ever and you can use it while continuing to eat any type of food you want.

My publisher was delighted. He was ecstatic. 'So, Paul,' he said to me, 'can you do another weight-loss book?'

'No,' I replied, 'that's it. I've put into that book everything I know that helps people lose weight. What's the point in writing another one? It would just be repetition.'

My publisher was disappointed. In fact, he was more than

disappointed, he was really upset. I'd written him a bestseller and now I was refusing to cash in with a sequel.

And for eight years that is the way it has been. I updated *I Can Make You Thin* in 2007, and in 2010 I produced a version with colour illustrations, but basically that was that.

So why am I writing this book? Why is there a need for another book about how to lose weight?

The answer is that in 2011 a medical friend introduced me to Dr Mark Cohen, an endocrinologist who specializes in treating obesity.

Obesity is a growing problem throughout the developed world and is strongly correlated with ill health. Being fat is not just a lifestyle choice, it puts you at serious risk of ill health and an earlier death.

One treatment for seriously overweight patients is gastric band surgery. Surgery is expensive and, although the risks of modern surgery are lower than ever, they are higher for seriously obese patients. Ironically, some of the people most in need of help are in fact too obese for surgery.

Mark had heard that some people were asking their hypnotherapist to convince them they had had a gastric band fitted. He asked me if I would cooperate with him on a trial so that he could compare the hypnotic gastric band with a surgical gastric band.

My first thought was that it sounded a bit like a gimmick. I was not sure, but Mark was very persuasive, so I agreed to discuss it further.

The first experiment

We decided to do a study as a precursor to a full clinical trial. I designed and recorded a hypnotic trance that created a hypnotic gastric band. It takes a while to set up a study, but as I had already recorded the trance, I decided to give it to a few people and get some informal feedback. The feedback was very quick and absolutely astonishing. Every single person who used the hypnotic trance lost weight. There were no exceptions.

But that wasn't all. A few weeks after we had completed the recording, I was talking to the sound engineer and he told me he had noticed he was enjoying his food as much as ever but he was eating less. Then he weighed himself and discovered he had lost weight. A week later the producer told me he had also lost weight. To top it off, I noticed that I too was eating less and I'd lost weight as well.

Now this evidence does not constitute a proper study or a controlled trial, but it was still remarkable. Every user lost weight. Even the people who worked on it, who had no intention of losing weight, lost weight. That proved to me that this hypnotic gastric band was extraordinarily effective.

The second experiment

Soon afterwards I was invited to appear on *The Dr. Oz Show*. Dr Oz is a practising cardiothoracic surgeon and his show is the most watched talk show in the USA. I suggested that he find me some of his viewers who wanted to lose weight and I would give them the hypnotic gastric band. That's what we did. As ever in TV, there was very little time to set things up and I was not able to meet the volunteers before the show. I just spoke to them on the phone and sent them *I Can Make You Thin* and the hypnotic gastric band trance.

Every single volunteer found him- or herself eating less, and even inside one week all of them lost weight. Women who would regularly eat large portions were leaving more than half their food on the plate.

A woman who regularly drank three or four large bottles of soda was drinking only one. Another woman who started to lose weight immediately had even experienced some transient pain in her abdomen, in the same way that people who have had a surgical operation do in post-operative recovery. Two women said they simply couldn't eat as much as before because they became nauseous. All of them were delighted. Nine months later, although one woman registered no significant change, another had lost fifty pounds and kept it off, and the third had lost seventy pounds.

Three out of ten

In a remarkably short span of time, I had accumulated a lot of evidence about how powerfully the hypnotic gastric band works. But equally I had research evidence that the system in *I Can Make You Thin* also works. As we saw above, seven out of ten people who read *I Can Make You Thin* lose weight. That is a fantastic statistic, a better long-term result than any diet, but it is not ten out of ten. What about the other three out of ten? What happened to them? Why didn't it work?

My research revealed that the most common reason that people did not lose weight is that they did not use the book properly. They only used the CD once. They didn't finish reading the book. They didn't follow the Four Golden Rules. Or they stopped after a week.

Interestingly, they gave a lot of different reasons why they stopped using the system properly, but they all boiled down to the same thing: they didn't follow the instructions.

Well, my mind was put at rest. If people don't follow the instructions, it is not surprising that it doesn't work.

However, I did find a small number of people who, it seemed, were willing to follow the rules but they just weren't very good at it. They claimed they were really trying to follow the Four Golden Rules but at the same time they kept eating until they became seriously uncomfortable. Specifically, they couldn't recognize when they were full.

Some of them had been overweight a long time; others

either were or had been bulimic. Some were very, very overweight. Some told me they felt addicted to fast food. They never felt completely satisfied by what they ate, so they kept wanting more of it.

Others seemed in every other way normal, but they just didn't seem to be able to catch the moment when they felt nicely full. They could feel hungry and they knew what it was like to feel stuffed, but they were not consistent in recognizing a comfortable feeling of having eaten enough.

That meant that something had gone wrong with their natural internal signalling system. If their body wasn't telling them when they were full, they needed some specific physiological help.

I realized that for some people a hypnotic gastric band was the perfect booster to help them tune into their own body.

As the hypnotic gastric band had a one hundred per cent success rate, I hypothesized that it was helping people in two ways:

1. **It restricted their eating.**
2. **Because they felt full much more quickly, it was amplifying the signals from their stomach, so people were finding it easy to eat less and easy to stop before they felt uncomfortable.**

That is why I decided that making the hypnotic gastric band available was a worthwhile addition to *I Can Make You Thin*. Some of those three out of ten people who did not lose weight really wanted to follow the Four Golden Rules, and the gastric band would help them succeed.

A hypnotic gastric band is not a substitute for following the Four Golden Rules, it is a physical change that makes it natural to follow them easily. The hypnotic gastric band and the rules go together perfectly because the band physically restricts your food intake, and the rules ensure that even though you eat less, you don't starve and you enjoy every mouthful.

A hypnotic gastric band is simply the most powerful way to launch you into a lifetime of healthy eating and maintaining a thin, healthy body.

A personal challenge

For the sake of completeness, I must also tell you I have one more reason for writing this book. I don't like losing. I know from the tens of thousands of people I have met at my seminars and from the millions of people who have successfully used *I Can Make You Thin* that the system works. Follow the instructions and you will lose weight. So it bothered me that the success rate was not a hundred per cent. It bothered me that some people appeared to be doing their best but not getting good enough results. That's why I always ask questions when people say they have had problems.

And that is also why, when the opportunity arose to create and test something this powerful, I followed it up. I want everyone to have a real alternative to being fat and being ripped off by the diet industry. If you want to lose weight, I want you to succeed.

How it works

The hypnotic gastric band allows you to reset the brain–body feedback system. By constricting the amount of food you can eat, you re-sensitize the stomach and it signals 'fullness' to you more clearly and quickly. The technical term for the feeling of fullness is 'satiety'. For a significant number of people, chronic overeating and continually overriding the body's natural signals of satiety appear to have taught the brain to ignore the satiety signals so that eventually they fail to have any impact. These people simply never feel full. They can even feel pain in their stomach from the amount of food they have crammed in and yet still not feel satisfied. They want to carry on eating because they have trained their brains to ignore the signals of satiety. It takes a radical hypnotic intervention to reduce the amount of food they eat and restore their natural sensitivity.

Don't try to believe

To install your hypnotic gastric band, all you need to do is follow my instructions accurately and completely. I will give you all the detail you need as you go through the book.

Incidentally, it is not necessary to try to believe in the process. Although all of the people who initially tested the hypnotic gastric band wanted to lose weight, most of them found it difficult to believe it actually could work. They just gave it a chance.

It was only when they found themselves full and satisfied after eating less than half of what they normally ate that they began to imagine it might really help them. They ate less, stopped snacking, left food on their plates and yet felt full and completely satisfied. Eventually, in spite of their initial, and in some cases total, scepticism, they realized that it works. So don't worry about what your conscious mind thinks or believes. Just follow the instructions below and let the hypnosis and your unconscious mind do the rest.

CHAPTER TWO

•

Your Nutrition
and the
Gastric Band

Your nutrition and the gastric band

Your body is a truly amazing machine. It generates all the energy you use. It keeps your heart beating and your lungs breathing twenty-four hours a day. It does all this using just the food you eat, the air you breathe and the energy it has stored in your body. At the same time it repairs and maintains itself without ever stopping work.

When we fit your hypnotic gastric band, that fuelling, repair and maintenance system continues to work just as nature intended, but there will be a few, very important differences:

1. **You will have less room for food in your stomach.**
2. **You will feel full sooner.**
3. **That 'full' feeling will be clear and urgent.**
4. **You are very likely to experience changes in your food preferences.**

As you are eating less, your body may be a bit more picky or seek out new foods to ensure it gets all the nutrition it requires. You don't have to worry about this with your conscious mind at all. You continue to eat just what you want, but you'll notice that what you want to eat changes. At first those changes may be quite subtle, so it may take you a little time to realize that you now find different foods attractive.

The magic of your digestive system

It will be helpful to have an overview of your digestive system so that you understand how your hypnotic gastric band works. Some people are curious and interested in how the body works, others are not. However, whatever you consciously think, it is important that you read this section so that your unconscious mind has all the information it needs to process my hypnotic instructions. So even if you find this section a bit complex, just keep going because your unconscious mind will understand and use all it needs from this explanation.

Your digestive system starts work as soon as you smell your food. Your salivary glands get to work so that when the food reaches your mouth there is already saliva to mix with it to make it easier to swallow and to begin to break it down.

Next, the physical motion of chewing your food sends signals to your stomach to release hydrochloric acid. When you swallow, the food goes down your throat, or in technical language your oesophagus. At the bottom of your oesophagus is a muscular valve called a sphincter which relaxes to let the food into your stomach. The sphincter protects your oesophagus from the acid in your stomach. Sometimes indigestion or overeating causes acid to get back up through that sphincter into your oesophagus. That creates the feeling we call heartburn.

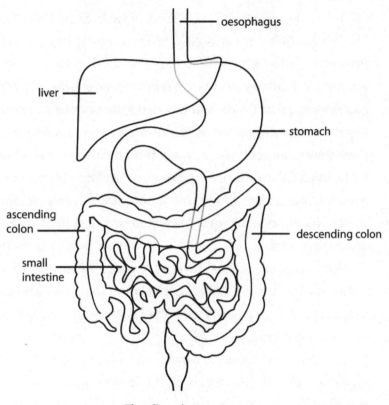

The digestive tract

In your stomach your food is mixed with acid and enzymes which break the food down into smaller particles. Proteins and fats take longer to process than carbohydrates, so different foods spend more or less time in the stomach. Vegetables can take less than an hour, and red meat can take several hours to process. Of course, you don't have to think about this, your body does it all automatically.

From the stomach, your food, now broken down into smaller particles, is released a bit at a time into your small intestine. It is only now, when the food goes into your intestines, that your body extracts the nourishment. More enzymes break it down into molecules that are small enough to get through the wall of your intestines into the bloodstream. Carbohydrates are broken down into glucose, which is taken to the liver. Glucose is used to power the muscles in your body. Proteins are broken down into amino acids and distributed via the bloodstream throughout the body and used to build and repair cells.

As the food passes through your intestines, all the nutrients are extracted, then in the colon the water and salts that helped the process are absorbed back into your body and the rest is excreted.

All these processes are organized by a set of hormones, or signalling chemicals, in your body. In your digestion one of the most important is called glucagon-like peptide-1 (known as GLP1). It is released as food enters your intestines. GLP1 does lots of different jobs. The two most important are:

1. **It signals to a part of your brain called the hypothalamus that you have had enough to eat.**
2. **It increases insulin secretion from the pancreas. The insulin links with the glucose going into your bloodstream and allows it to be stored in your muscles and liver.**

Because GLP1 does both these jobs simultaneously, the feeling of fullness is linked to the process that gets energy into your muscles. This ensures that you don't feel full until your body is getting all the energy it needs.

Levels of another hormone, called peptide YY (known as PYY), also increase when you have eaten. PYY reduces appetite and increases the efficiency of nutrient absorption, so again it links stopping eating to making sure you get what you need.

Levels of a third hormone, called ghrelin, decrease after a meal. Ghrelin is one of the hormones that make us feel hunger. It also stimulates parts of the brain necessary for learning, so being hungry is linked to learning new things, such as new ways to find food, or liking new types of food.

Scientists are continuing to find out more and more about how our hormonal system works, and this pattern of one hormone doing two or more jobs is very common. Over and over again we discover that two jobs are linked in a way that promotes health and survival.

Alongside the hormones, your body also communicates to your brain through the nervous system. When your stomach fills up, the stomach wall is stretched and nerves in the wall react and send electrical signals to the brain.

All of these systems work very elegantly together, but they get thrown out of balance by overeating. When people eat too much, the body believes there must be an important reason why its signals are being ignored, and assumes the overeating is a deliberate preparation for a famine that is about to happen. So all the extra food is converted to fat, which is basically stored energy.

When your hypnotic gastric band is fitted, it stops that overeating, and as you move towards a healthy weight your normal responses to your hormonal and nervous signals are restored.

The power of the gastric band

Your stomach is about the size of a melon. When it fills up, you feel full. A gastric band fits like a collar around the top of your stomach and it creates a pouch a bit smaller than a tennis ball. When that pouch fills up you feel full and you simply can't eat any more. It is as though your stomach has become ten times smaller.

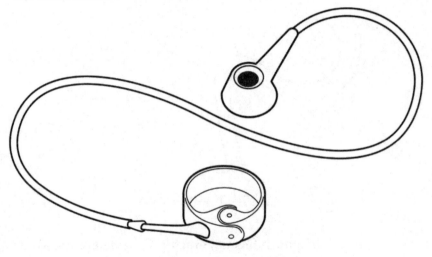

A gastric band

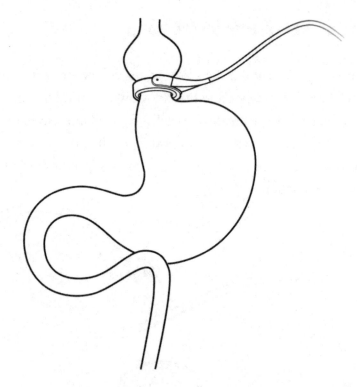

A gastric band in place

When the pouch fills up, exactly the same hormonal and nervous signals are triggered as when your whole stomach was filled up, so you feel full in exactly the same way. With your gastric band, you reach satiety, that feeling of fullness, much more quickly.

The gastric band creates a very narrow opening from the pouch into the rest of the stomach. The band has an inflatable ring on the inside that is inflated with saline solution to adjust the size of the opening. It is set so that the food very slowly

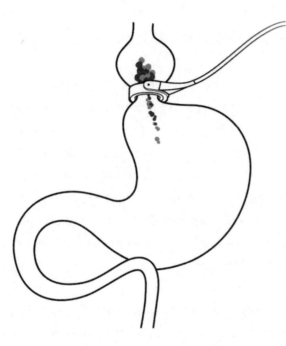

A gastric band in place with trickle of food going
down into lower section of stomach

passes through this opening and then goes through your
system in the usual way.

Because the space in your stomach is now so much
smaller, you physically can only eat a small amount. It can
become uncomfortable to try to eat too much. Luckily you
don't have to eat so much that you get uncomfortable because
the gastric band makes your body signal 'full' as soon as that
pouch is full.

The preparation for gastric band surgery

If you were having the physical operation, you would meet your surgeon for a consultation before the surgery. The surgeon is obliged to explain the risks of the surgical operation. The biggest single risk of any surgery is the formation of a blood clot, most often in the legs, which goes through the bloodstream to the heart. There are other potential complications from the anaesthetic and surgical procedures. These risks are greater for more obese patients. Fortunately, with a hypnotic gastric band, all these physical risks are eliminated.

The surgeon would also explain to you the best way to prepare for your operation. The surgeon will make two recommendations for all his patients.

1. He will recommend that they walk for at least twenty minutes a day. This ensures the circulation is healthy and reduces the risk of a blood clot forming post-operatively.
2. He will recommend that for one to two weeks before the operation they abstain from high-sugar and high-fat foods: in other words, broadly speaking, fast foods and processed foods. The reason for this is very specific. High-fat and sugar foods make the liver work hard and fill it up with glycogen. That makes it expand. The part of the stomach where

the band will be fitted lies directly beneath the
liver, so when they eat less fat and sugar for a couple
of weeks, the liver shrinks and makes access to the
stomach easier for the surgeon.

The operation

The operation to fit a gastric band takes about an hour and is conducted under general anaesthetic. The operation is laparoscopic. 'Laparoscopic' means that instead of making one large incision and exposing a large part of your insides, your surgeon makes four or five small incisions. In one of them, he inserts a tiny TV camera with a light and uses it to guide the other instruments with which he inserts the gastric band.

He carefully manoeuvres the band into position around the top section of your stomach and locks it into place. Next

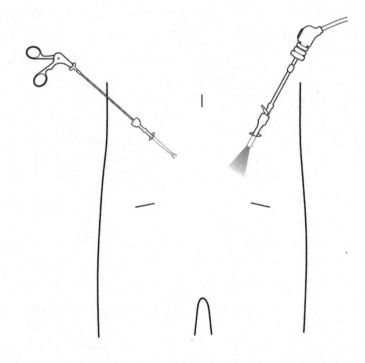

he runs a thin tube from the band to a port which is placed just under your skin in your lower abdomen. Using a special needle he can inject a saline solution into that port and inflate the ring inside the gastric band to adjust the size of the opening. After the band has been in place for a week or so, the surgeon will use the port to inflate the balloon inside the band to ensure the gap is the correct size.

At the end of the operation the surgeon removes all his instruments and stitches up the cuts he has made. He can do this so neatly that when the scars have finished healing they are barely visible.

When you wake from the anaesthetic there may be a small amount of discomfort but it soon passes. There is no need to stay at the hospital. You can go home on the same day.

Post-operative instructions

After a physical operation the surgeon will advise you that there are three things you can do to maximize the benefit of your gastric band.

1. **Don't drink with meals. This means your food doesn't pass through the opening too fast, so you feel full more quickly.**
2. **Avoid soups, casseroles and smoothies. With my system and your hypnotic gastric band you can of course eat anything you want when you are truly hungry, but if you have a choice, choose something else. The reason is the same. More solid food allows you to feel full more quickly.**
3. **Remember to chew your food thoroughly. This allows time for signals from your mouth to prepare your stomach so that as your stomach fills up you quickly feel full.**

Disadvantages of a surgical gastric band

Gastric band surgery has been done for many years so the surgeons are very experienced, and the newer types of band used nowadays have vastly reduced the risks of slippage or puncture, which occurred with earlier versions. The operation is now very safe. Nonetheless, every surgical operation carries some risks, and these risks, in particular the risk of blood clots, are increased with seriously overweight patients.

The other major disadvantage of physical surgery is cost. It can cost several thousand pounds to have the operation.

Both of these disadvantages are eliminated with the hypnotic gastric band.

CHAPTER THREE

•

Preparing for your Hypnotic Gastric Band

Preparing for your hypnotic gastric band

The hypnotic gastric band works in just the same way as the physical one: your intake of food is restricted by your body so that you feel satisfied after very modest meals. There are just three key differences between the physical and the hypnotic band.

1. With a hypnotic band all adjustments are automatically done by continued use of the trance.
2. With the hypnotic band there is no physical surgery, and hence no physical risks.
3. The hypnotic band is many thousands of pounds cheaper.

How hypnosis improves communication between stomach and brain

How do you know when you have had enough to eat?

First, you can feel the weight and location of the food. When your stomach is full, the food presses against and stretches the stomach wall and the nerve endings in the stomach wall react. As we saw in Chapter Two, when these nerves are stimulated, they send a signal to the brain and we get the feeling, 'I have had enough.'

Secondly, as the stomach fills up and food enters the intestine, PYY and GLP1 are released and trigger a sense of satisfaction in the brain that also prompts us to stop eating.

Unfortunately, when people chronically overeat, they become desensitized to both the nervous signals and the parallel neuropeptide signalling system. During the installation trance, we use hypnosis and imagery to re-sensitize the brain to these signals. Your hypnotic band re-establishes the full impact of these nervous and neuropeptide messages.

With the advantage of hypnosis we are able to recalibrate this system and increase your sensitivity to these signals, so that you feel full and really satisfied as soon as you have eaten enough to fill that small pouch at the top of your stomach.

A hypnotic gastric band makes your body behave exactly as though you have undergone the surgical operation. It constricts your stomach and alters the signals from your stomach to your brain so you feel full quickly.

The hypnotic band makes use of several extraordinary characteristics of hypnosis. First of all, hypnosis allows us to talk directly to parts of the body and mind which are not under conscious control. Incredible as it may seem, in hypnosis we can actually persuade the body to behave differently even though our conscious mind has no means of directing that change.

The power of hypnosis

A famous and dramatic example of the power of hypnosis to affect our bodies directly is in the emergency treatment of burns. Dr Dabney Ewin, the Clinical Professor of Surgery at Tulane University in New Orleans, has used hypnosis hundreds of times to speed up and improve the healing of severe burns and to reduce the pain for his patients.

If someone is severely burned, there is tissue damage and the body responds with an inflammation. Dr Ewin hypnotizes his patients and prevents the inflammation. His patients heal more quickly and with less scarring.

There are many more examples of how the mind can directly and physically affect the body. We know that chronic stress can cause stomach ulcers, and a psychological shock can turn someone's hair grey overnight. However, what I particularly like about Dr Ewin's work is that it is a clearly documented example of how the mind affects the body in a positive and therapeutic way.

It truly is a miracle of the human being that thoughts and hypnosis can cause profound physical changes in your body.

In fact, hypnotic trance all by itself has a noticeable physiological effect. The most immediate effect is that subjects find it deeply relaxing. Interestingly, the most common observation that my clients report after I have seen them – regardless of what we have been working on – is that their friends and family tell them they look younger.

Cybernetic loop

Your brain and body are in continual communication in a cybernetic loop: they constantly influence each other. As the mind relaxes in hypnosis, so too does the body. When the body relaxes, it feels better, and it sends that message to the brain, which in turn feels better and relaxes even further. This process reduces stress and makes more energy available to the healing and immune systems.

It is important to note that the therapeutic effects of hypnosis do not require trickery or amnesia. All of Dr Ewin's patients know they have been burned, and he does not ask them to lie to themselves. He simply hypnotizes them and asks them to imagine cool, comfortable sensations over the affected area. That imaginative activity changes their body's reaction to the burn. The enzymes that induce inflammation are not released, and as a result the burn does not progress to a higher level of damage and there is minimal pain during healing.

By using hypnosis and visualization, Dr Ewin gets his patients' bodies to do things that are completely outside their conscious control. Willpower won't make these kinds of changes, but the imagination is stronger than the will. By using hypnosis and visualization to talk directly to the unconscious mind, we can make a physiological difference in as little as twenty minutes.

In my own work I recently had another extraordinary illustration of how hypnosis can speed up the body's natural healing process. I worked with a soldier in the special forces who suffered from severe episodes of eczema. He told me that the fastest recovery he had ever made from an eczema episode was six days. I knew that the process of healing is a natural sequence of events run by the body, so I hypnotized him and in trance asked his unconscious mind to follow the exact same procedure that it normally uses to heal his eczema, but to do it all faster. One and a half days later his eczema was healed.

With hypnosis we can massively enhance the effect of the mind upon the body. When we fit your hypnotic gastric band, we are utilizing exactly the same system of hypnotic communication to the unconscious mind. We communicate to the brain with vivid imagery and the brain modifies your body's reactions, altering your physical reaction to food so that your stomach is constricted and you feel really full after just a few mouthfuls.

What makes the hypnosis work so well?

Some people find it hard to believe that hypnosis and imagery can have such an extreme and powerful effect. Some of Dr Ewin's medical colleagues initially were sceptical and believed that his patients must have been less severely burned than was recorded, because the cures he effected appeared to be near miraculous. It took several years and many remarkable cures before his work was widely understood and accepted.

Sometimes, of course, the sceptic and the patient are the same person. We want the results but we struggle to believe that it really will work. At the conscious level, our minds are well aware of the difference between what we imagine and physical reality. However, another amazing hypnotic phenomenon demonstrates that it doesn't matter what we believe at the conscious level because hypnosis allows our mind to respond to a reality that is completely independent of what we consciously think. This phenomenon is called Trance Logic.

Trance logic was first identified fifty years ago by a famous researcher of hypnosis called Dr Martin Orne, who worked for many years at the University of Pennsylvania. Dr Orne conducted a number of experiments which showed that in hypnosis people could behave as though two totally contradictory facts were true at the same time. In one experiment he hypnotized some people so they could not see a chair he put directly in front of them. Then he asked them to walk straight ahead. The subjects all swerved round the chair. However, when questioned about it, they insisted there was nothing there. They could not see the chair. Some of them even denied that they had swerved at all. They believed they were telling the truth when they said they could not see the chair, but at another level their body knew it was there and moved to avoid hitting it.

The experiment demonstrated that hypnosis allows the mind to operate simultaneously on two separate levels, believing two separate, contradictory things.

It is possible to be hypnotized and have a hypnotic gastric band fitted and yet to 'know' with your conscious mind that you have not got surgical scars and you do not have a physical gastric band inserted. Trance logic means that part of your mind can believe one thing and another part can believe the complete opposite, and your mind and body can carry on working, believing two different things are true. So you will be able consciously to know that you have not paid thousands of pounds for a surgical operation, and yet at the deepest level of unconscious command your body believes that you have a gastric band and will act accordingly. As a result, your stomach is stimulated to signal 'feeling full' to your brain after just a few mouthfuls of food. So you feel satisfied and you lose weight.

Visualization is easier than you think

The hypnosis we use to create your gastric band uses Visualization and Affect-Laden Imagery. Visualization is simply the creation of pictures in your mind. We can all do it. It is part of thinking. For example, think of your front door and ask yourself which side the lock is on. To answer that question you see a picture in your mind's eye. It doesn't matter at all how realistic or bright the picture is, it is just the way your mind works and you see as much as you need to see.

Affect-laden imagery is the psychological term for pictures that are emotionally meaningful. In this process we use pictures in the mind's eye which have emotional significance. Even though hypnotic suggestions are powerful, they are dramatically enhanced by powerful images when we are communicating directly to the body. For example, you may not be able to speed up your heart just by telling it to beat faster, but if you imagine standing on a railway line and seeing a train rushing towards you, your heart speeds up pretty quickly. Your body responds very powerfully to vivid, meaningful pictures.

That is why I will describe your operation in the trance section. It doesn't matter whether or not you are listening consciously, your unconscious mind will hear all it needs to replicate the real band, in just the same way that a vivid picture of an approaching train affects your heart rate.

You do not need to hold the images of the operational

procedures in your conscious mind, because of course during an operation you are anaesthetized and unconscious. Regardless of what you consciously remember, beneath the hypnotic anaesthesia your unconscious mind uses all this information and imagery to install your gastric band in precisely the right place.

The power of context

Contextual cues are another significant component of hypnotic suggestion. For example, when I performed my hypnotic stage show, the context of the theatre, the lights, the stage and the expectations of the audience all enhanced the hypnotic phenomena, regardless of whether the participants were consciously aware of it.

The same is true with the gastric band. I outlined in the last chapter the preparation that surgeons require before the physical gastric band operation, and it is important that you follow the same preparatory procedure as well. This replicates the physical context for the operation within your own body. That makes it even easier for the hypnosis to have an immediate, powerful effect and embed the changes you need to make into your body.

The surgeons ask their patients to walk at least twenty minutes a day. If you add up all the walking you do in a day, almost all of us already do this. Only a few very inactive people walk less than this. However, if you want, you can make absolutely sure you do it by making a point of taking a particular walk of twenty minutes, for example by walking to the next bus stop or down to the local park and back. The point of the walking is not fitness or exercise but just ensuring good blood circulation in the legs. When you do it, your preparation for your hypnotic gastric band is identical to the preparation for a surgical gastric band.

A positive side effect, however, is that it will set you up for the exercise that your body will want to do when you lose weight. This may seem odd to you now, but as you reach your natural healthy weight, you will become one of those people who are naturally thin and fit and actually enjoy walking and many other sorts of exercise.

The second preparation that surgeons request is that their patients abstain from high-fat and high-sugar foods for a week or two before the operation. Basically this means eating less fast food. This begins to reduce the liver back to its normal size, thus making the stomach more accessible. Again, it creates a powerful and compelling contextual support when you do exactly the same thing before installing your hypnotic gastric band.

As with the twenty minutes of walking, there is a positive side effect here too. The body's digestive system is adapted for natural sugars in fruits and plants. Refined sugar gets into our bloodstream much faster, so our bodies go into overdrive and create extra insulin to carry the sugar to the liver and muscles. Quite often, however, there is even more insulin than sugar, so our blood sugar levels go from too high to too low – and that causes us to crave sugar, or fast food, again. That is why, a short while after gorging on burgers or cakes, overeaters crave more of the same. They are going up and down on the seesaw, but never balancing in the middle.

This seesaw contributes to drowning out the natural signals of satiety or fullness. Going from low sugar to high sugar and back again is such a powerful swing that some people don't notice the natural, gentle signals from their stomach telling them, 'You've had enough.'

When you stay away from fast food for a week or two, you give your body a chance to get used to a longer period of natural balance, and those natural signals become obvious again, so it is easier to tell when you have had enough. Then whenever you do eat fast food, your body finds it much easier to re-establish equilibrium afterwards.

After your operation you can eat whatever you like, whenever you feel hunger, although you will only be able to do so in small amounts. Remember, naturally slim people eat hamburgers and chocolate and chips, they just don't eat them to excess, because they can discern the signals that tell them, 'You've had enough.'

Of course, with your hypnotic gastric band those signals will be very loud and clear, and you simply won't be able to eat so much. But the great advantage is that you will also feel completely satisfied.

IN A NUTSHELL

To establish the correct context for your
hypnotic gastric band operation:

1. **Make sure you walk at least twenty minutes a day.**
2. **Before you use the Gastric Band Installation
    Trance, don't eat high-fat and high-sugar food.**

After your band is fitted, you are free to eat whatever you
want, but notice the changes – see the next chapter!

CHAPTER FOUR

•

Your New, Thinner, Happier Life

Your new, thinner, happier life

It is very important that you read and use this chapter before you fit your hypnotic gastric band. You need to adjust your self-image, your behaviour and your feelings to fully enjoy and benefit from your new slim body. If you don't prepare yourself, there is a chance you could feel uncomfortable or confused, and fail to enjoy the benefits of losing weight permanently.

So read this chapter carefully, and as you lose weight you will feel happier and more confident and you will have all the tools you need to deal with the new situations that arise.

As soon as your hypnotic gastric band is fitted, your life will change. You will eat less and lose weight, but you will also experience a cascade of changes that will affect every area of your life. You will also be participating in an even bigger change that is sweeping through society. You will be part of the movement away from diets towards genuine healthy weight loss. From now on you will eat differently, but you will not be dieting, because diets don't work.

Diets don't work

Dieting makes the body think the person is starving, so the longer they diet, the more they end up bingeing. By the time they reach their target weight, their body feels it has been starving for ages, so as soon as they relax it fights back and gets them to go straight into a pattern of overeating.

The scientific research is clear and incontrovertible. The vast majority of dieters lose weight only temporarily, then they put it back on. Worse still, more than 70% end up heavier than when they started. No wonder there is now a worldwide army of doctors who are moving against the diet industry and diet clubs. For more than 90% of people, diets don't work! The diet industry insiders have known this grim truth for years and yet still they hawk their money-making schemes. And even though the evidence of failure is all around us, people keep starting diets.

Guilt

One of the reasons many overweight people struggle on and on with diets is guilt. At some level they believe their excess weight is their own fault. They feel guilty, so they think they deserve the suffering of denying themselves nutrition and pleasure from food. These people start out feeling bad, and then because dieting doesn't work they feel even worse.

I certainly do not believe anyone is a bad person because they are overweight. If you are overweight it is not your fault, it is the fault of your programming. You have had bad programming installed that has simply unbalanced the natural system of enjoyment and nourishment from food. I absolutely know that you can lose weight and feel good and enjoy the process.

Gambling

Another reason that millions of people go on diets over and over again is the law of intermittent reinforcement. This is the same reason why people become addicted to gambling. The fact is that although in the long run a gambler always loses, he does occasionally win. However, he never knows exactly when he will win. The possibility that this time he might win keeps him betting just one more time. This is the intermittent reinforcement. It is the same with diets. Almost all people lose weight in the first month of a diet and they keep hoping that on *this* diet the weight loss will continue. And just occasionally, very occasionally, it does. We all know at least one or two people who have managed to lose weight in spite of all the problems of diets. Dieters tend to look at them – the fewer than 10% who are successful – instead of the 90% who fail.

I don't believe in gambling. I believe in a rational, scientific approach to life. My approach to weight loss and my hypnotic gastric band are based on the best available evidence to date. Seven out of ten people who use my weight-loss system lose weight and keep it off. The hypnotic gastric band increases that success rate to more than nine out of ten.

Diet promotion

Diets are relentlessly promoted all around us. Indeed, some of the diet clubs now study my marketing messages and try their best to copy them, even though they are selling something completely different.

Diet organizations also pay celebrities millions of pounds to endorse them. They make a deal with an overweight celebrity and as part of the package they have someone follow them around monitoring their food to make sure they slam off the weight in time for the January pictures in the magazines, where these rich and famous people can talk about their struggle with their weight. Well, anyone would find it easier to stay on a diet if they had a team of people controlling their food intake. Diet clubs also seek out a certain kind of doctor, someone who is prepared to endorse them and in return be very well paid.

I was approached by these diet clubs years ago when I started pointing the finger at them, to see if we could 'work together'. Well, I double-checked the research then and I confirmed the facts. When people use my system properly in the long-term, it works. When people diet in the long-term, it doesn't work. I could see why they wanted me to endorse their products but there was nothing in it for me or for you. It would have been dishonest.

In the years since then I have frequently asked diet clubs to join me on a televised debate to talk about the merits and success of our different approaches to weight loss. In all those years they have never managed to take up my invitation, in spite of all the free publicity it represents.

Ironically, diet clubs are not in the weight-loss business. They do create camaraderie with their weekly meetings, and that is actually a very good thing because it is great to have support when you are on a mission. But the meetings are not their real source of profit. They are really a way to keep people involved and close to their products. As members become less successful at losing weight through willpower alone, they become more susceptible to buying products that promise miracles. And the diet clubs make their real money selling low-fat chemically modified food and food substitutes. They are in the artificial food business.

Hostile

Some people have asked me why I am so hostile to the diet industry. Why don't I just shut up and accept that different people have different approaches to weight loss? The answer is that I feel very strongly about the subject. I feel indignant on behalf of all the people I have met in my weight-loss seminars who have suffered for years using diets that made them feel guilty and a failure, and still left them overweight.

If diets just didn't work that would be bad enough. But it's the fact that they leave so many people even heavier than before they started that gets me really worked up. I believe a principal reason why we now have 60% of people in the UK and USA overweight is decades of dieting. Diets and diet clubs are the problem!

Looking at the science, there is a better case for banning diets than banning smoking. Diets and diet clubs are causing massive amounts of misery and ill health, putting a huge burden on our nation's health-care system. Starving your body gives you the illusion that the diet is working, whilst you are losing muscle mass not fat (totally the wrong kind of weight), and at the same time slowing your metabolism. They are killing you, they know it, and all they can think about is profits!

When I see someone overweight, I don't just see layers of fat, I see layers of frustration, caused by a group of cynical money-makers, who don't care for the people they exploit, nor about the damage they are causing to the lives of the people they are supposed to be helping. So when the diet clubs steal my slogans when talking about weight loss, it just makes me more determined to expose them and show as many people as possible how easy it is to lose weight.

Stop worrying about food

I have gone on a bit about diets for two reasons. One, as you can see, is that I am passionate about the topic. The second is that if you have ever dieted in the past you are now going to change your eating habits drastically. Your hypnotic gastric band will help you lose weight and you will now need to eat differently so that you enjoy your new body and don't undermine your happiness with the habits of dieting.

Dieters worry about food. They automatically divide food into 'good' and 'bad'. On diets they think about food almost all the time – except when they are eating, when they bolt their food and feel guilty.

You are not dieting so you can stop worrying. You are not going to overeat, so you can get hungry, eat properly and really enjoy it. Do not starve yourself. Those days are over.

You no longer have to be frightened of food. You can stop thinking about it when you are not eating. Now you can get hungry properly and eat properly. That means you really feel the body's natural desire for food and really satisfy it, all safely protected by your hypnotic gastric band.

A little while ago I was on television talking about food and a woman called in and said, 'I want to thank you for helping me escape from food prison.' I asked her what she meant by that. She explained, 'I used to count calories, I weighed myself every day and I thought about food constantly. Your system has helped me to realize that my weight naturally goes up and down a little, I don't have to panic and I don't have to diet. I'm slimmer than I ever was and I enjoy my food.'

She had found out that having a slim, healthy body is not an ordeal. It is a natural, satisfying way of life.

Life changes

When you lose weight your whole life changes. Because you have a hypnotic gastric band you will not be able to overeat, so it is absolutely vital that you prepare yourself for all the changes that are heading your way. Even the best things in the world bring challenges and we need to learn how to handle them, and your success is going to have very significant consequences.

For example, it is easy to think, 'Oh, I wish I could live in a really smart house', and certainly it would be very nice to have all the space. But you also need to learn how to look after it! If you don't want to spend all your time cleaning it you'll have to learn how to employ the right people and how to get on with them working all around you.

You also would need to deal with some other things that you might not think about at first, such as the different ways people treat you, and your property, when you live in an impressive house. It is not always easy – the papers have regular stories about lottery winners who have troubles coping with all that their money has brought them. That comparison is not extreme. In fact, losing weight will change your life in a far deeper and more positive way than winning a ton of money or trading up to a multi-million-pound house.

THE FOUR GOLDEN RULES

Even though you may have instant success with the hypnotic gastric band, it's important that you use the Four Golden Rules that are the foundation of my system. They help to support the changes you are making.

You might wonder why you need the golden rules now that you have a hypnotic gastric band, but in fact those rules are at the heart of all the healthy eating of all naturally thin people. Naturally healthy people eat when they are hungry, they eat what they want, they pay attention to their food and enjoy it, and they stop eating when they are full.

In other words, **healthy slim people follow the Four Golden Rules naturally. It is the natural, healthy way to eat.**

The brilliant thing about your hypnotic gastric band is that it creates the physical changes that make it natural for you to follow the golden rules too. Let's remind ourselves of them right now.

GOLDEN RULE 1

WHEN YOU ARE HUNGRY, **EAT!**

When some people hear me say this, they think it's crazy. They say, 'That's the problem, I can't stop eating, now he's suggesting that I eat.'

What I am saying is that only when you are truly *physically* hungry, eat. If you starve yourself, your body goes in to 'survival mode' and you slow your metabolism. So when you are truly hungry and you eat, your body knows there will always be enough food, so it doesn't slow the metabolism and you have enough fuel in your engine to do the things you need to do.

It's very important to make the distinction between real physical hunger and emotional hunger.

Real hunger comes on gradually. It is clear and constant and you feel it in your belly. It is not triggered by anxiety nor by an emotional pang that comes on suddenly when you feel upset. It is not a reaction to fear, embarrassment or anger. It is not an idea to distract you when you are bored.

Real hunger is a simple physical feeling in your stomach. Sometimes we mistake emotional discomfort for hunger. We imagine if we eat, we will feel better. But food doesn't fix emotions, it just covers them over temporarily. There are many far better ways to deal with emotions than eating. In fact, in the next chapter I will teach you a technique called Havening, which is an amazingly efficient way of addressing any painful or uncomfortable feelings. I have also included a DVD in this system so that I can guide you through the Havening process personally, step by step. If you suspect you want food because actually you feel bad, you can use Havening to feel better and then check in with your body and discover whether you are really physically hungry.

Recognizing real hunger

Proper physical hunger is a specific physical feeling and with your hypnotic gastric band you will find it easier than ever to recognize it. It will also be easier to recognize when you are really full. But for the sake of complete clarity and to make sure that you are accurately oriented at both conscious and unconscious levels, I'm going to ask you to do a small thought experiment that will help you instantly and easily to recognize the signals for when you are truly hungry and when you are full. If you have ever toughed your way through a diet, you will have distorted your response to your body's natural signals. This exercise will help your mind to re-calibrate your stomach's natural sensitivity to hunger and satiety.

1. **Think of a time when you were really, really hungry – so hungry you felt faint and even a crust of stale bread would have tasted delicious. Remember that.**
2. **Now think of a time when you were absolutely stuffed – when you'd feasted and eaten so much you were in pain, even nauseous. Remember that.**
3. **Do this several times so that you emphasize the difference between being starving and stuffed.**
4. **OK, now relax. Those two feelings are the extremes. You never have to feel either of those awful feelings again. You never have to be that hungry and you never need to feel that full.**

I have devised a scale where 1 is so hungry you are faint and 10 is so full you feel you will explode. It will help you to recognize easily where your body is at any time.

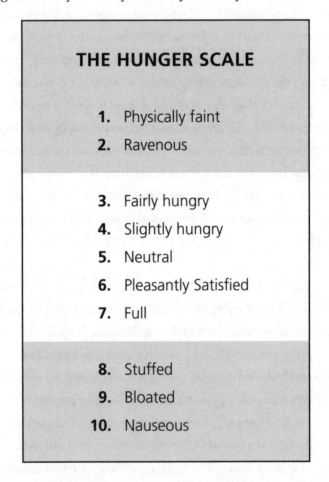

THE HUNGER SCALE

1. Physically faint
2. Ravenous

3. Fairly hungry
4. Slightly hungry
5. Neutral
6. Pleasantly Satisfied
7. Full

8. Stuffed
9. Bloated
10. Nauseous

From now on, NEVER go below 3 or above 7 ever again!

As you find it becomes easier to live in the middle section of the scale, your relationship with food and your body will change for the better. You will feel more in control, and like anything you practise for a few days, it will soon become second nature.

With your hypnotic gastric band, every single one of these stages will be as clear as daylight.

When you are between 3 and 4, it is time to eat.

When you are between 6 and 7, it is time to stop eating.

With your hypnotic gastric band, you cannot eat as much as before, so as soon as you feel full, stop eating. Don't try to eat more, because it will hurt to try to squash more food into your stomach.

GOLDEN RULE 2

EAT WHAT YOU WANT,
NOT WHAT YOU THINK YOU SHOULD

As soon as you make a food forbidden, it becomes all you can think about. That's why with your gastric band and with my system there are no forbidden foods. You know what it's like to think, 'I must not have chocolate cake ... I must not taste that sweet, rich, delicious cake.' It's game over. You end up having it and beating yourself up.

That way of eating is like fighting with your body. It is like driving a car by flooring the accelerator and hauling on the handbrake. It is a waste of fuel and it trashes the car. This syndrome is amplified by dieting. Dieting distorts your body's natural systems.

All diets involve limiting and depriving the body. So the body's response is to crave high-energy emergency foods to make up the deficit as quickly as possible. That is why people on diets all dream about high-fat, high-sugar foods like cakes and crisps and chips and ice cream. The more they diet, the more they want those foods. There is nothing wrong with any of them, by the way – but as you move away from dieting towards balanced nutrition you may be surprised to notice that what you want to eat begins to change. As you become more sensitive, food that you never paid attention to starts to appeal to you. You will also notice that you begin to favour fresh food, even when it takes more time to cook or prepare. This happens because your body is no longer trying to rescue you from starvation. It is not looking for an emergency energy fix. Now it is free to move towards greater health. As you lose weight it seeks out the protein, vitamins and minerals it needs to tighten and clarify your skin and build your muscles.

The great thing about all these changes is you don't have to think about them at all. Your body's natural wisdom will guide you. The more you pay attention to your body, the more you will realize that hunger is not just a simple need for energy. You will begin to notice you are hungry for a specific food, such as fish, or salad, or cake. You will notice you prefer one vegetable to another, and so on.

To sum up, dieters eat what a book tells them they should eat. Healthy people eat what their body really wants.

GOLDEN RULE 3

WHENEVER YOU EAT, DO IT **CONSCIOUSLY**

This is possibly the most powerful piece of advice I can give you and what I am about to tell you is now supported by numerous scientific studies around the world. When I say eat *consciously*, I mean two things:

1. **Pay attention to what you are eating and nothing else. Give your food your complete attention. Focus on the food and NOTHING else!**
2. **Slow your eating speed right down. Slow down to about a quarter of your previous speed and chew each mouthful twenty times.**

When people eat fast they flood their brains with happy chemicals and they can't hear the signals from their stomach that say, 'You are full.' So they end up out of control and over-eating. It's very important that as you chew each mouthful of food, you put your knife and fork down and *chew your food twenty, yes, twenty times*!

If you can't do this, I don't think I can help you and I don't believe anyone can. It's a small ask with a massive reward.

Focus on your food

You can eat whatever you want, whenever you want, so long as you give it your complete, undivided attention. That means never, ever eat and do something else at the same time. When you eat, sit at a table, eat your food from a plate, using a knife and fork, and chew your food at least twenty times.

This may seem a little over the top to you now, but it is absolutely vital to retrain yourself to totally pay attention every second you are eating. This will ensure that you really enjoy your food. Savour the taste and texture of your food and really notice it as you swallow it and feel how it fills your stomach.

By paying attention to eating, you will find it simple and easy to notice the satiety signal that you receive from your hypnotic gastric band, and you will stop eating and be completely satisfied long before you would have expected to because you will actually feel how quickly your stomach fills up.

This is the one thing I need you to do to make totally sure you can experience the benefit of your hypnotic gastric band and lose weight. Unconscious eating is how people lose track of their body's natural weight-control system in the first place. By eating consciously, you respect your food and you respect yourself.

Research has shown conclusively that people always eat more when they watch television. Focus on your food exclusively. That means not only no television, but also no reading while you eat. Don't surf the internet or answer emails or text your friends. Do not drink alcohol when you eat because it dulls your attention and distracts you from the actual food. Don't grab snacks while driving or listening to music or playing a game or using your phone.

That may sound demanding but it is also amazingly helpful. Because it means that you should only ever eat food that you completely enjoy.

Slow down

Giving your food your full attention and eating slowly means it is really important to enjoy every mouthful. When you really, really slow down, you will notice that some types of food you used to enjoy are not so pleasant to you now. This is entirely natural. Now that you are not slamming food into yourself, your body has time to signal to you what it really needs for true nourishment.

When you eat slowly, you give yourself the chance to notice and appreciate your food and you give your body a chance to react naturally so that you clearly feel the signal of fullness as soon as it is triggered.

I really emphasize eating consciously because so many people do not realize how little they notice their food and how little they get from it.

Now that you are not worrying, and you are eating what you want when you are really hungry, your food will taste better than ever. And that is as it should be. You are eating much less so every mouthful is precious and every mouthful should be delicious.

This is the one thing you have to do: when you are eating, *slow right down and pay attention* so you are absolutely and completely focused on the activity of eating and feeling the food in your mouth and your stomach.

I am emphasizing this over and over again because even though it is actually rewarding to pay attention and enjoy your food, it is a new habit. You are leaving behind an old behaviour that you may not even have noticed you had. This change means you don't grab something and eat it walking down the street. You don't graze on snacks while working or reading or watching telly.

Where food is concerned, you do one thing at a time. You can't give your full attention to your food when you are doing something else. Make sure you eat only when you have a real meal, when you sit at a table to eat.

If you are eating with friends or family, don't eat and talk at the same time. It is polite not to talk with your mouth full, but more importantly, if you are eating you should be paying complete attention to your food.

Don't graze during the day. Do eat at proper mealtimes, and sit at a table to eat. Don't eat on a couch in front of the television.

Put the knife and fork down while you are chewing your food and *really* enjoy it. Savour the taste, and enjoy the wonderful textures and sensations as you chew each mouthful of food thoroughly. Chew each mouthful twenty times. The principle behind these instructions is to create a habit of paying attention to your food. Having meals sitting at a table creates a healthy environment and positive associations which build your appreciation of food and respect for yourself. That will mean you not only lose weight but you enjoy your food properly, perhaps more than ever before.

Occasionally people say to me that they imagine it looks

a bit strange eating slowly and chewing their food twenty times. I tell them that actually it is quite common. Many slim people naturally eat like that. And it is a lot more attractive to see someone eating slowly and enjoying themselves than shovelling food into their mouth at high speed.

The more you pay attention to your food, the more you enjoy it, and the more satisfied you feel even when you are eating so much less. You can eat whatever you want, whenever you want, so long as you fully enjoy every single mouthful.

GOLDEN RULE 4

WHEN YOU THINK YOU ARE FULL, **STOP** EATING!

I know this sounds like common sense, but it's important to say it. Fast eating floods the brain with the happy chemicals released by eating and drowns out the signals of satiety from the stomach. Basically it anaesthetizes the pain of overeating. Now that you have slowed your eating speed and got rid of distractions like the TV, you are free to hear that signal more clearly than ever before. It's like a muscle: the more you use it, the stronger it gets.

Some people think they don't know when they are full. In which case it's perfectly OK to wait and see. Other people say, 'But what if I am hungry ten minutes after I have stopped?' Well, that's easy: follow Rule 1: When you are hungry, EAT!

The brilliant thing about your hypnotic gastric band is that it gives you a clear, unmistakable signal from your stomach as soon as you are full. Some people who have dieted too much have confused themselves by anxiety and calorie-counting and portion control and all sorts of other unnatural ways of ignoring their body's wisdom. Some are so confused that they have even lost touch with the natural cycle of nutrition. They diet and control themselves, then binge and try to ignore it, then go back to dieting, and so on and on.

Your body is naturally designed to use the energy in your food, and as your stomach gradually empties it builds up a hunger signal for you. At a certain point that signal becomes clear and steady. You know you are hungry. By the way, if an emergency happens, you won't die if you don't eat. If a fire breaks out before you get to eat, you will have plenty of energy to run away, fetch water and put out the fire. But when you are definitely hungry, you know it is time to eat. And when you eat the nutrition your body needs, it lets you know by releasing the neurochemicals of pleasure. When you have eaten enough, you get the satiety signal and you know it is OK to stop eating.

Dieting made a mess of that simple, natural cycle. Your hypnotic gastric band will help you get it back. It amplifies the satiety signal, that comfortable feeling of satisfaction in your tummy. Your stomach feels full but not taut and you notice that you are not really keen to eat any more. Your body feels lively but relaxed and comfortable, and you feel satisfied. That is satiety and it is there to help you stop eating before it becomes uncomfortable.

Nowadays there is no need to eat extra food because we are not being threatened with starvation. Your body will take a few hours to digest what you have eaten and then begin to build a hunger signal again. This simple, natural cycle will look after you for the rest of your life. All you need to do is follow it. Feel real hunger, eat good food, and feel comfortably satisfied.

If at first you are not quite sure if you are feeling the satiety signal correctly, stop eating for three or four minutes and see if you are still actually hungry. If you are not hungry, you got it right and you will feel relaxed. If you are still hungry, eat and watch out for the signal again.

And when you are full, stop eating. Even if you leave food on your plate, your body will be perfectly happy with that. Gradually you will get used to helping yourself to a bit less when you sit down to eat.

Enjoyable eating

The Four Golden Rules are how healthy, slim people eat naturally. They are the simplest way to get the most enjoyment and satisfaction from your food as you lose weight with your hypnotic gastric band. They also ensure that you continue to get all the energy and nourishment you need as you lose weight and when you arrive at your natural, healthy, slim weight. They are very easy to follow.

I have talked to people at my weight-loss seminars who tell me all sorts of reasons why they think they just can't follow the Four Golden Rules. There are mums with children to feed and look after, working mums with no time to shop for fresh food, and busy executives who travel around the world. There are all sorts of excuses people make to themselves for not eating in a healthy way or not making time for themselves.

But I also meet people who have all those things to deal with, children, busy jobs, lots of travel – even allergies and health issues – who manage to follow the Four Golden Rules. Because in fact all we need to do is tune into our body's natural wisdom.

If you are not hungry, then any impulse to eat is really an attempt to deal with something else – an emotion such as boredom, fear or anxiety. Food never really deals with those feelings, it just covers them up. I'm going to show you how to deal with those feelings properly in the next chapter.

CHAPTER FIVE

•

An Astounding
Breakthrough

An astounding breakthrough

I have helped people all over the world to lose weight. The Four Golden Rules combined with the hypnotic gastric band can now help absolutely anyone achieve a healthy body weight.

But for each of us there is one question: what caused us to become overweight in the first place? We all have a built-in natural system to regulate our weight and keep us healthy. How come that system got overridden? For each person there is at least one, if not more, reasons why they over-ate.

I have heard people tell me all sorts of reasons why they were overweight: 'My job was stressful.' 'Losing my job was stressful.' 'Being a mum was stressful.' 'Not being a mum was stressful.' 'I don't have time to eat properly.' 'I have too much time on my hands.'

For every reason I've heard for being overweight, someone else claims they are overweight for the exact opposite reason. The truth of the matter is all of them are right. Different people have different reasons why they over-ate. But if all the reasons are different and some are even completely opposite, do they have anything in common? The answer is yes!

Serotonin

Whatever the external circumstances, whatever their background and whatever the triggers, physiologically there is one reason why people eat too much: they are trying to feel better. Specifically they are trying to trigger a serotonin release. Serotonin is a hormone that our bodies release which makes us feel good.

People who don't feel good enough in themselves live in a state with chronically low serotonin. Their basic state has been set at the wrong level. It is like a central heating system which has a faulty thermostat – you can override it to heat the place up, but as soon as the automatic system kicks back in it gets too cold again. Our bodies are a bit more complicated – but not much.

There are two particular hormones that have a very important role in governing our behaviour and internal state: serotonin and dopamine. Dopamine makes us active and alert – it promotes movement, thinking and focus. In basic evolutionary terms it drives us to seek food and shelter. When we have achieved our goals, serotonin is released and creates a good feeling that rewards us for our efforts.

When all is going well, we have a decent amount of serotonin being released. When a goal is in sight, dopamine is released to mobilize us and help us focus and learn what we need. When we achieve our goal, serotonin is released again. This cycle carries on throughout our lives. It is the chemical basis of our experience as we strive for and achieve our goals. There are, however, two ways it can go wrong. The first is known as 'hyper-vigilance'.

Hyper-vigilance

Hyper-vigilance is the state in which we have a higher than usual amount of dopamine in our bloodstream, and we never fully experience a sense of achievement. Nothing is ever quite good enough. We never fully relax and give ourselves a complete dose of serotonin. Even when we do succeed in achieving something, we immediately find something else to worry about.

This condition is created when we have been in a stressful situation for such a long time that we have learnt to be permanently vigilant, because we feel that something could go wrong at any point.

There are many, many causes of this state. It could be an emotionally or physically abusive childhood. Equally it could arise in a very loving childhood, but one in which the child is always expected to achieve something and never gets enough space in which to simply play. It could be a difficult relationship, or an excessively demanding job.

Whatever the situation, it was one in which a stressful environment lasted for so long that it became the norm and our survival instinct reset our 'thermostat' to a hyper-vigilant high-dopamine state.

This state causes people to seek serotonin continually. Consuming food leads to a temporary increase in serotonin, which feels good, but as the base state is hyper-vigilance it reverts swiftly to high dopamine and the cycle starts again. This is the chemical situation behind many addictive behaviours. Whatever the addiction – food, drugs, alcohol, pornography, shopping – it is a temporary source of serotonin which gives relief from hyper-vigilance.

Learned helplessness

Ironically, the opposite state, in which people do not have enough dopamine, creates exactly the same problem. People living with a base state of too little dopamine have a state known as 'learned helplessness'. In this state it feels as if whatever they do, it will make no difference.

They have low serotonin, so they don't feel good, but they also have low dopamine so they have low motivation to change the situation. They feel stuck. Eating will cause a temporary increase in serotonin, so for a little while it provides a good feeling – but as soon as the serotonin wears off, they revert to a low-serotonin, low-dopamine state and the person feels flat, low and unmotivated again. Just like too much dopamine, too little dopamine can cause people to fall into addictive behaviour, to food or anything else that causes a temporary rise in serotonin.

The problem with eating too much is that as a solution it only works temporarily. It is a short-term answer to a long-term problem. And of course becoming overweight then leads to poor health and other problems.

Havening

We need to raise our serotonin levels directly, consistently, and without negative side effects. My good friend Dr Ronald Ruden MD Ph.D. has created the Amygdala Desensitization Technique, which does exactly that. His technique is more commonly known as Havening.

Havening allows people to reduce stress and increase serotonin in a matter of minutes. What is even more wonderful is that if people consistently use the Havening technique along with other activities to address the underlying issues, over time the base level of serotonin is gradually increased. Day by day their average level of contentment is raised.

Below I'm going to explain how Havening works and take you through the process step by step. However, just before I do so, I want to make two more points.

First, as soon as your hypnotic gastric band is installed, you will be eating less food and you will be losing weight. As you eat less, the old way of raising your serotonin levels is no longer available. You will get more serotonin by ensuring that you consciously enjoy every mouthful, but you will no longer be able to keep producing serotonin simply by eating more and more. So to feel good you must use this Havening technique.

Secondly, as soon as you lose weight you become more sensitive. That means being more sensitive to all your feelings, whether they are comfortable or not. The more sensitive you are, the more important it is to maximize your good feelings. Once again, it is vital that you use this technique so that you have a pleasurable experience of losing weight.

Incidentally, you may have noticed that this is why the standard diet-club way of losing weight is so painful and inefficient. When people think about food all the time but eat low-calorie diets, they lose weight but they don't do anything about their base levels of serotonin, so they experience deprivation. And if they are eating chemically modified milkshakes instead of proper food they are being doubly deprived.

When you follow the Four Golden Rules, you will enjoy your food and lose weight. When you use Havening, you will enjoy the whole of your life, more and more. Scientific studies have shown that it is amazingly effective at relieving sadness and reducing stress, trauma and compulsion.

Dr Ruden's technique is a breakthrough in the field of psycho-sensory therapy. He discovered that patterns of repeated touch to parts of the body combined with specific eye movements and visualizations have a rapid, reliable and predictable effect on our feelings. The patterns of touch used in Havening are the patterns that a mother uses to comfort her baby. They are hardwired into every infant.

Havening combines these deep-rooted patterns of reassurance and comfort with cognitively significant sensory sequences to break down the associations that trigger unhappy feelings. As a result, in just a few minutes we can now reduce the intensity of an emotion or feeling of unhappiness and establish calm, robust relaxation.

This technique is not merely a distraction. Studies have shown that when we use the Havening technique, we reduce stress chemicals in our body and produce states of relaxation and calm. We therefore change the way our brain processes thoughts and feelings. The effect of the specific sequence I will share with you is to reset the way your brain interprets and responds to stress. Over time this actually alters the neuronal pathways in your brain.

This technique is so important that I have filmed a short video in which I illustrate it and take you through it step by step. That video is on the DVD included in this book.

However, I have also written out the technique, step by step in the box below. Read it now and use the DVD as well.

The best way to use Havening is to practise it so often that you know the whole sequence off by heart. It doesn't matter whether you use the written instructions below or the DVD, so long as you practise it so thoroughly that you can do it easily whenever you need it.

A SAFE HAVEN

Please read through the following exercise before you do it. You should practise this sequence of eye movements, body touches and visualizations over and over again until you have memorized it. If you suffer from motion sickness, do not do the eye movement, but you can use all the other elements of the process. When you have memorized it, you will be able to use it any time you need to get rid of unhappy feelings and swiftly feel calm and relaxed.

Start by noting how much unhappiness or sadness you feel and rate it on a scale of 1 to 10. This is important as it lets you measure how much you reduce it.

1. Now clear your mind, or just think about something nice.
2. Next, use both hands to tap on both your collarbones.
3. While you continue tapping on both your collarbones, look straight ahead, keep your head still, close your eyes and open them again.
4. Continue tapping, keeping your head still, and look down to the left then down to the right.
5. Continue tapping, keeping your head still, and move your eyes in a full circle clockwise and then anticlockwise.
6. Now cross your arms, place your hands on top of your shoulders and close your eyes.
7. Now stroke your hands down the sides of your arms from your shoulders to your elbows, down and up, again and again.

8. As you carry on stroking the sides of your arms, imagine you are skipping over a rope or, if you prefer, walking on a beach, and count out loud from 1 to 20 with each step you take.

9. When you reach 20, hum 'Happy Birthday'.

10. Now, let your arms drop and relax them, and open your eyes and look up in front of and above you.

11. Move your eyes slowly from left to right and back 3 times.

12. Close your eyes and stroke the sides of your arms again 5 times.

Open your eyes and check, on your scale from 1 to 10, the number of the feeling now. If it is way down the bottom, congratulations – you have personally changed your own feeling state. If you think the unhappy feeling is not yet reduced enough, just repeat the Havening sequence until it is reduced as far as you want it to be.

When you are learning this, you can keep referring to the points above, or do it with me on the video. Go over it until you can run the whole sequence from your own memory. Then you will have it available at any time of day or night.

When people first see these instructions, some of them think it looks a bit complicated, and some don't believe it could possibly help. It just seems too strange that a sequence of gestures and motions can make such a fast and yet profound change to such deep-seated emotions.

Havening really does create a rapid and profound change in how you feel. And of course, because the brain and body are completely interlinked, it changes your body too. I was visiting Dr Ruden once and mentioned to him that I had a bad pain in my back. He suggested that we use Havening. I pointed out that it was a physical pain in my back, not an emotional problem. Ron reminded me that the brain and body are interlinked. He guessed that my bad back was stress-related. We did some Havening and in fifteen minutes my back was no longer stiff or painful and I felt so much better.

But don't take my word for it. Don't try to believe it. Just do it. Follow the instructions to the best of your ability and notice how much it changes your feelings.

CHAPTER SIX

•

A Whole New World

A whole new world

You know that when you have a natural, healthy, slim body, you will feel happier. You will be pleased with your achievement. You will use Havening to ensure that your serotonin levels stay high and you will be fitter and healthier. Is there really anything else you need to know?

Yes. And no. For some of you, that is all you need. You are going to carry on, lose weight, enjoy life and be happy to face the challenges it offers. However, all these changes will have further consequences and some of you will find things go a lot smoother with a bit of preparation.

I'm going to run over a few of those consequences and some useful ways to meet them so that you can relax and fully enjoy your weight loss. It may be that in the end some of this does not apply to you, but just in case it does, it is worth reading.

Energy

When you lose weight, you will have more physical energy and your body will crave exercise. The first part of this seems wonderful: who wouldn't want more energy? You can get more done and have more fun. But craving exercise? That may seem rather unlikely. Lots of people think of exercise as an unpleasant chore, a nasty, uncomfortable ritual that people go through in their painful struggle to get fit. That is another belief created by the diet-club conspiracy. You can get all the exercise you need having fun and you never need to go to a gym or go running. If you like the gym of course you can go there – but most of us don't. We find it boring.

The fact is that your body has muscles and they evolved to be used. We no longer have to chase and kill animals to survive, but our bodies feel better when they are fulfilling their natural function. As you give up carrying excess weight, you will notice a spring in your step and a new liveliness. That is your body waking up.

A few people have worried that if they do vigorous exercise it might disturb their gastric band. There is no need to worry. Your hypnotic gastric band will not be moved by exercise. If it needs adjustment as you burn even more energy, it will be done automatically when you next listen to the installation trance.

Whatever your lifestyle, as your body lightens up, you will relish the opportunity to use your muscles. It could be cycling to work or walking at the weekends. It could be swimming or sailing or chopping wood. It could be karate or drumming or dancing or hula-hooping or mountain-climbing. It could be anything from athletics to zumba.

You may have absolutely no idea what activities you will enjoy doing. Again, that doesn't matter. Just try something, anything, and if you like it, do more. If you are not sure, do it again until you are. If you don't like it, do something else. Just experiment until you get a genuine, enduring sense of fun. You are looking for a physical activity which you really enjoy doing.

For many of us this is completely contrary to the ideas we have grown used to having in our heads. I have a good friend who took up mountain-biking. I remember when we were kids, the bit we really liked was speeding downhill. We moaned about pushing our bikes uphill and screamed with excitement when we came down. My friend told me that one morning he was cycling up a steep track and was absolutely astonished to realize he was enjoying himself – cycling *up*hill! He was enjoying the sensation of power in his muscles.

The point of this exercise is not to get fit or to lose weight. That is going to happen anyway. The point is to discover how to use the energy you are releasing in a way that is rewarding. So instead of feeling agitated, nervous or confused, you will feel lively, excited and motivated.

Whatever you do, remember to take it easy at first. You are looking for an experience that is enjoyable and rewarding.

If it doesn't make you happy after a little while, move on and find another activity that does.

One more reason for building some form of physical activity into your lifestyle is that it will mean that re-setting your base level of serotonin will happen more quickly. You are now activating another set of neurotransmitters by creating and releasing physical energy. Exercise releases adrenalin, and when you finish exercise, the body releases endorphins. Both of these will help your body to raise your serotonin levels.

Time

You will have more time. This is nothing to do with the time that is spent eating. Maybe now that you are paying attention to every mouthful and really enjoying it, you take longer to eat, and you might be doing more cooking for yourself as your taste buds seek out foods laden in minerals and vitamins.

Regardless of how long your meals take, you will have more time because you'll spend less time worrying about food or diets or weight. And you will also *feel* that you have more time, because food will become simpler and yet be more delicious. If you are hungry, you will eat. You will enjoy every mouthful. And time flies when you are enjoying yourself.

If people have time and nothing to do, sometimes they get bored. And some people eat when they are bored. You physically won't be able to eat that much any more, so if ever you are bored it is important to know what to do, because food is not an option.

Just in case you need it later, I'm going to ask you now to write out a list of things you would love to do if you had all the time in the world. Would you like to plan a round-the-world trip? Do you want to learn another language? Is there a sport you want to play? Would you like to improve your memory, or play a musical instrument? Or learn to juggle? Start a list of all the things you would really, really love to do if you had all the time in the world. Don't put any limits on the list. Write down all the things you'd like to do, regardless of time or money or opportunity. Write down absolutely everything you want to do, whether it's learning to knit or flying an aeroplane.

After your hypnotic gastric band is fitted, you may find a few odd moments of the day when you feel at a loss. You won't be snacking or worrying about food and maybe you don't know what to do. Pull out your list and find the first thing you can do on that list. If you only have ten minutes to spare you can't suddenly set sail around the world – but you can read about navigation. Even if your list is full of all the most outrageous, expensive things you can imagine, there is always one small step you can take in the direction of your dreams. If you want to fly a jet, you can practise on a computer simulator. If you are learning to dance, you can practise some steps while waiting in a queue or rehearse them in your head. Use your new time to begin to realize your dreams. And step by step, moment by moment, you can use the new freedom and energy you have gained from losing weight to begin to realize your dreams.

More attractive

As you become slimmer, you will appear more attractive to the opposite sex. This seems like a winner, doesn't it? More people will appreciate you. What's not to like? Well, it will be pleasant, but again it brings challenges.

A good number of the people, mostly women, whom I have helped to lose weight over the years, have told me that one of the advantages of being overweight was that they did not have to deal with the attention of men.

If people you like but don't fancy come on to you, how do you deal with it? How do you say 'no' without hurting their feelings? If you are not used to being attractive and suddenly lots of people hit on you, how do you keep your feet on the ground and choose the right one? And when you have chosen someone, how do you deal with the fact that all the others still keep chasing you?

You may think, 'I should be so lucky', but sooner than you realize, this is the sort of thing you will have to deal with. So let's start practising now. I have two simple but powerful exercises that will transform your sense of self.

STEPPING INTO THE MORE ATTRACTIVE YOU

Read through this whole exercise before you do it so you know what to do. Find somewhere you can be undisturbed for five minutes, and when you are ready, begin.

Think about someone you consider to be attractive, confident and happy with their body. It could be a friend or colleague or it could be a movie star, it doesn't matter.

1. Stand up, close your eyes and imagine the person you think of as attractive standing in front of you, and you standing just behind them. You can see the back of their head in front of you.

2. In your mind's eye, examine them carefully. How do they stand? What is their posture? Notice the way they hold their arms and shoulders and every detail of how they are.

3. Now take a physical step forward and imagine stepping into their body. Stand the way they stand, copy their body posture as best you can, hold yourself the way they do, and notice the confidence they feel in themselves.

4. Notice where they feel their good feelings about themselves most strongly. Is it in the head, the chest, or somewhere else? Notice where that feeling is in yourself.

5. Now imagine giving that good feeling a colour. What colour would it be? Give the feeling a colour and a shape within you.

6. Now imagine spreading that colour all the way through your body, from the top of your head down to the tip of your toes, until you feel bathed in this feeling of confident attractiveness.

7. Finally, imagine experiencing that feeling within you in all the situations of your everyday life. Run a video in your head of a typical day and see yourself looking that confident and feeling that good throughout your life now.

The more often you repeat this exercise, the easier it is for your mind to generate these good feelings. A feeling is an electrical, chemical event inside you, and through the power of your mind and imagination you are instructing your unconscious mind and body how to feel. And like any skill, the more you practise it, the better you get. Do it several times again now. Imagine taking that good feeling into all the areas of your life.

THE EYES OF LOVE

I believe that beauty is not just about how someone looks. It is way more than that. I have met people who look pretty on the outside but are certainly not on the inside, and I have met people who are not supermodels but have such an inner beauty that it shines through.

This next exercise increases your beauty from the inside. Once again, read through this whole exercise before you do it so you know what to do. Find somewhere you can be undisturbed for five minutes, and when you are ready, begin.

1. Close your eyes and think about someone who loves and respects you.

2. Imagine that person is standing in front of you now, looking at you and smiling.

3. Next, imagine floating out of your own body and into theirs, and look at yourself through their eyes. See yourself through the eyes of love and respect. Feel the smile on their face as they look at you. Notice how you smile in return.

4. Notice all the things they love and respect about you. Take all the time you need to do that. Notice absolutely everything, even the little things, that you can see. Notice how it makes you feel.

5.   Finally, take a snapshot of yourself in your mind and imagine seeing it up to the right in front of you.

6.   Keep this feeling and any time you want to be reminded of it, look up to your right and see that picture again.

Eating differently

My *I Can Make You Thin* system tells you that you can eat whatever you want so long as you eat SLOWLY and CONSCIOUSLY enough to truly enjoy every mouthful. I have run weight-loss seminars for many years, and on each occasion I send people out at their first lunch break and tell them, 'Eat absolutely whatever you want, but eat *consciously* – enjoy every single mouthful.'

After lunch I always ask people for their experiences, and without fail I get two responses. The first is, 'It was delicious! I've never enjoyed my lunch so much – but I couldn't finish what was on my plate!'

The second is, 'It was terrible! I ordered the sort of food I usually have for lunch but it was so boring. It didn't taste as good as I remembered.'

The first group of people are eating food their body enjoys and they have begun to listen to their satiety signals properly again. The second group of people have been eating food that is basically dull but loaded with sugar, fat and salts. As they are now eating consciously they notice, as if for the first time, how uninspiring that food is.

As soon as you fit your hypnotic gastric band, your tastes will change too – because now you are free to enjoy your food, and your body will seek maximum nutrition. You don't have to try to make this happen – it happens in its own time.

It happened to one of the first people to test our hypnotic

gastric band and she was very puzzled. When I called to check how she was doing, she was delighted to report the weight loss but she couldn't understand why she was eating different food. 'I used to eat lots of takeaways,' she told me, 'but now I'm cooking fresh vegetables. I don't really understand that.' I reassured her she was simply responding to the new healthy signals from her own body.

I don't know what sort of changes will occur in your eating habits, but there will definitely be changes, even if you don't consciously notice them at first. Maybe you enjoy your food more now that you sit down at a table to eat instead of eating in front of the TV. Maybe changes will happen but it takes several days or even a week or two before you become aware that, for example, you no longer eat snacks between meals. All you need to do is to follow the instructions of this system and be willing to accept the changes that your body prompts you to make.

Being different

As you are now eating differently, a few things will change in the rest of your life. If you were accustomed to eating while watching telly with your family on the sofa, they will have to get used to you eating at a table. They might want to join you, they might not – but whatever their decision is, you know that you will be most comfortable and successful when you are able to pay full attention to your food by eating at a table and not watching the television. For some people, and for some families, that will be a big change. Whatever your friends or family do is up to them – but what and where and when you eat is up to you. Just follow the Four Golden Rules and quietly do your own thing, and if they carry on in the old way, that's fine, just let them. Even if you feel a bit funny at first, eating a meal at a table on your own, just carry on. There is a good chance the others will join you in their own time when they see you losing weight and they see how much your life improves.

Changing your eating and changing your body size is so fundamental that it sets off a whole series of other changes. If ever you feel you need to pause and take on board all the changes, you will find that Havening is amazingly helpful. And remember, however much you change, it only happens one day at a time. One day at a time things will get better, and each improvement is a change.

Change – even change for the better – can be a challenge,

and it is astonishing how people become accustomed to a life less wonderful than we are truly capable of. Remember not to be too hard on yourself as you adapt to living a fuller life. When you lose weight, you are not really giving anything up – you are actually taking up a brighter, richer, more exciting life.

Success one day at a time

This system harnesses your own body's natural tendency towards health. In a way, it is like putting a bandage on a wound. The bandage doesn't do the healing, it just keeps the wound safe and clear of infection while the body's natural mechanism heals you. My system simply prevents you from overeating so that your body can restore your natural, enjoyable appetite for food and your organic sensation of pleasure and fulfilment. It really feels great to relax and know you have eaten enough.

Fitting your hypnotic gastric band is like turbo-charging your weight-loss programme. However, as you still follow the Four Golden Rules, you stay safely in touch with your body's natural need for nourishment.

Your hypnotic gastric band will have an immediate effect but the hypnosis also ensures that you maintain healthy nutrition throughout your weight loss. That means that the rate at which you lose weight will vary. Some weeks you will lose several pounds, other weeks you may lose just one pound or even less. The next week you may lose several pounds again. Because each of us has a slightly different body, the process is different for each of us as the body is continually adjusting to its new state.

Miraculous

All these changes may seem miraculous to you at first, especially when you begin to feel the physical effects. One of my earliest users of the hypnotic gastric band had been overweight since her childhood and had never, ever, *ever* lost weight in her entire life. She was absolutely astounded to find that less than a week after fitting her hypnotic gastric band, she was losing weight.

I'd like to share with you one thing I said to her. I told her, 'The best thing you can do now is to allow yourself to feel optimistic. Start getting used to things going well for you. And if they don't go well today, remember to feel optimistic that they will go well tomorrow.'

By following my system and fitting the hypnotic gastric band, losing weight for her was easier than she thought possible. However, she did have to put a bit of effort into changing her mindset to a positive one. She did that work, because after years of quietly feeling bad about herself, it was a big shift for her to move towards self-approval and optimism.

No one is perfect all the time and nothing goes well from start to finish. We all have to face obstacles and setbacks. But when we learn to be optimistic, progress becomes easier, obstacles become smaller and the journey itself becomes more and more enjoyable.

You are now on your way to your natural, slim, healthy

body weight. Start enjoying that fact right now. It will help you relax and enjoy the process even more. There will be days when you experience frustration and days when you need to practise patience, but the habit of optimism will help you accept your own success more swiftly and more easily.

So carry on now to the next stage of this system. Every day from now on is a step towards a healthy, slim body and a happier you! Enjoy the journey and prepare yourself to enjoy fully your new, thin body!

NEXT STEPS

Step 1

You have now read the whole book. That is correct, isn't it? You haven't just skipped to this page? If you haven't read the whole book, please go back and READ IT ALL THROUGH, at least once.

Follow the pre-operative instructions on page 67 and practise the exercises on pages 116, 128 and 130.

Step 2

Have you watched the Havening DVD? If you haven't, watch it now and practise the technique until you can do it without the prompts from me. This may take several goes and even several hours, but you must do this.

Even if you are perfectly happy with your life, you need to learn the Havening technique because it is a guaranteed healthy way to help you feel good.

Many overweight people eat not because they are hungry but because it makes them feel better. It is a way of managing their emotions. When you lose weight and you are not using food to feel OK, you need another way to feel OK.

With your hypnotic gastric band in place, you won't be able to use food simply to make you feel good. From now on you need to do it directly from your own resources. Havening is how you can do that, so learn the technique.

Step 3

Now listen to the pre-operative CD. You will notice that some of the information that you hear on the CD is new and some of it is the same as the information written in the book. Even when you hear something you think you know, keep listening! Your brain processes information you hear differently from information you read. We need both these pathways in your brain to receive this information to ensure your unconscious mind can use it all when it installs your hypnotic gastric band. By using both the literary and the aural channels, we are able to fully prepare your mind and body for your hypnotic gastric band. So listen to the CD all the way through. You don't have to concentrate with your conscious mind or try to remember it all. So long as you listen to it, your unconscious mind receives all the information it needs.

Step 4

Find somewhere you can be undisturbed for half an hour and listen to the Gastric Band Installation Trance. Try to avoid strenuous exercise for the rest of the day.

Step 5

Follow the Four Golden Rules every day and remember to eat consciously. If you forget or make a mistake, don't worry, you don't have to be perfect. Just keep going, follow the golden rules again and you will find that gradually over time they become second nature to you, just as they are to all the other people who are used to being slim and healthy.

Step 6

Listen to the Gastric Band Installation Trance at least once a month until you have maintained your target weight for at least six months. Your mind and body will then adjust the band to make the pouch a little smaller or a little bigger, so that you can continue to lose weight healthily and yet ensure you receive adequate nutrition.

Step 7

Enjoy your new life and your new thin body!

I look forward to seeing the end of diets and anxious, overweight people, and seeing more and more people healthy, happy and slim.

Until we meet,

Paul McKenna

I would like to say thank you to the following people:
Dr Natheera Indrasenan, Dr Mark Cohen, Dr Ron Ruden,
Dr Michael Carmi, Dr Mehmet Oz, Mike Osborne,
Kate Davey, Doug Young, Alex Tuppen, Mari Roberts,
Julia Lloyd, Robert Kirby and, of course, Hugh Willbourn
for his extraordinary effort on this project – and also to
all the people who were prepared to give this
breakthrough new system a chance.